Dixieland musicians

music notation

male vocalist/guitarist

Latin musicians

banjoist

drum set

2

jazz musicians

female vocalist

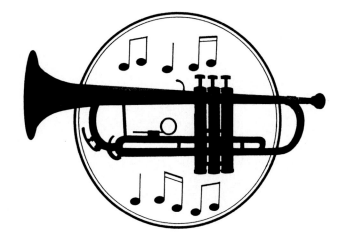

trumpet

3

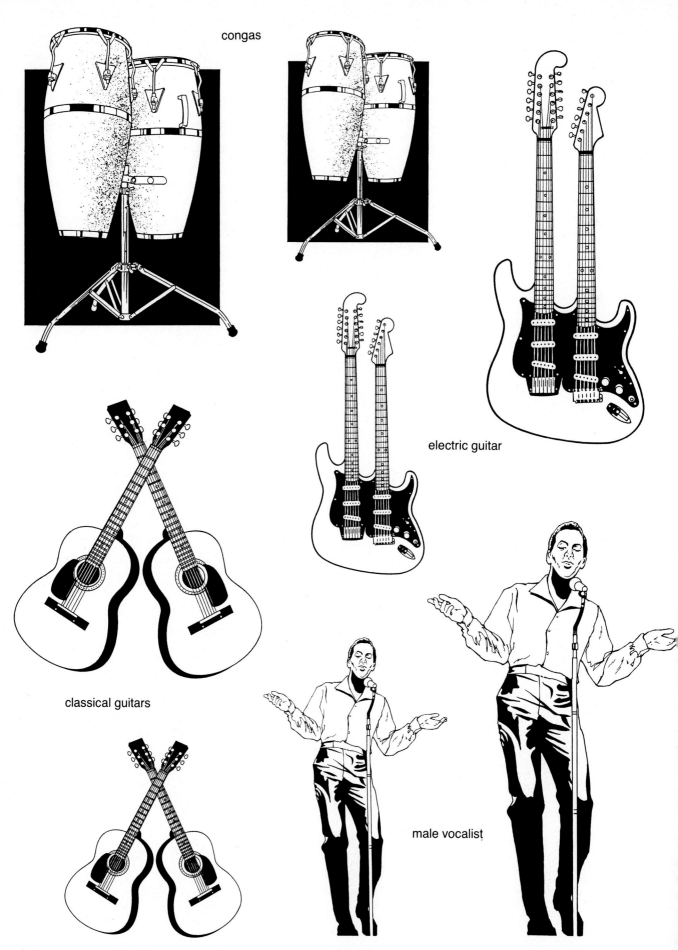

congas

electric guitar

classical guitars

male vocalist

4

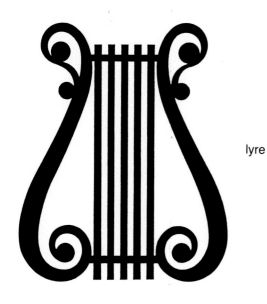

lyre

alto saxophonist

rock musicians

electric guitarist

trombones

pianist

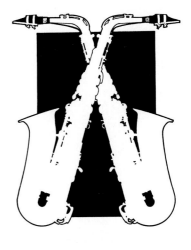

alto saxophones

gospel vocalists

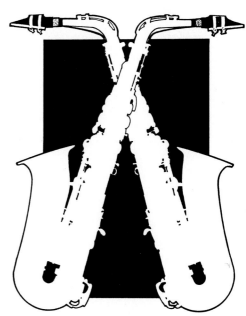

banjoist

country musicians

tenor saxophone

female vocalist

Cajun musicians

jazz musicians

electric piano

rock guitarist

bongos

jazz musicians

jazz musicians

blues guitarist

flute

11

baby grand piano

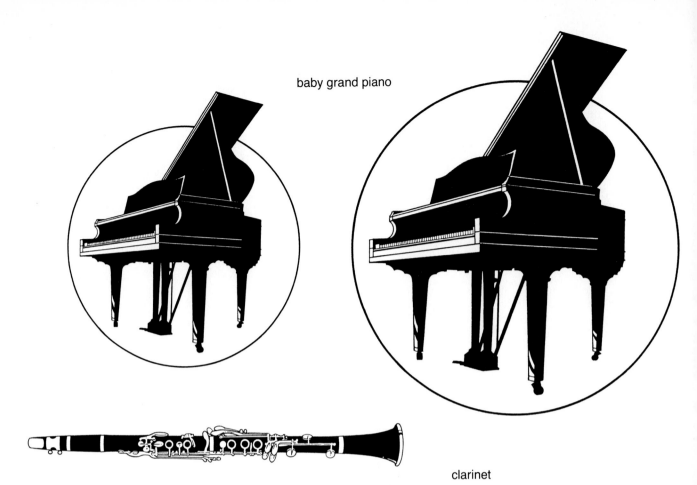

clarinet

drummer

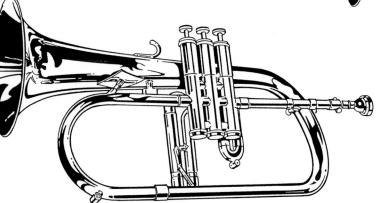

fluegelhorn

barbershop quartet

folk guitarist

trumpeter

bass bugle player (marching band)

jukebox

snare drummer (marching band)

wedding musicians

trombone

15

electric guitarist

female vocalist

spinet

16

electric guitar

rock musicians

17

klezmer musicians

tenor saxophonist

electric guitars

18

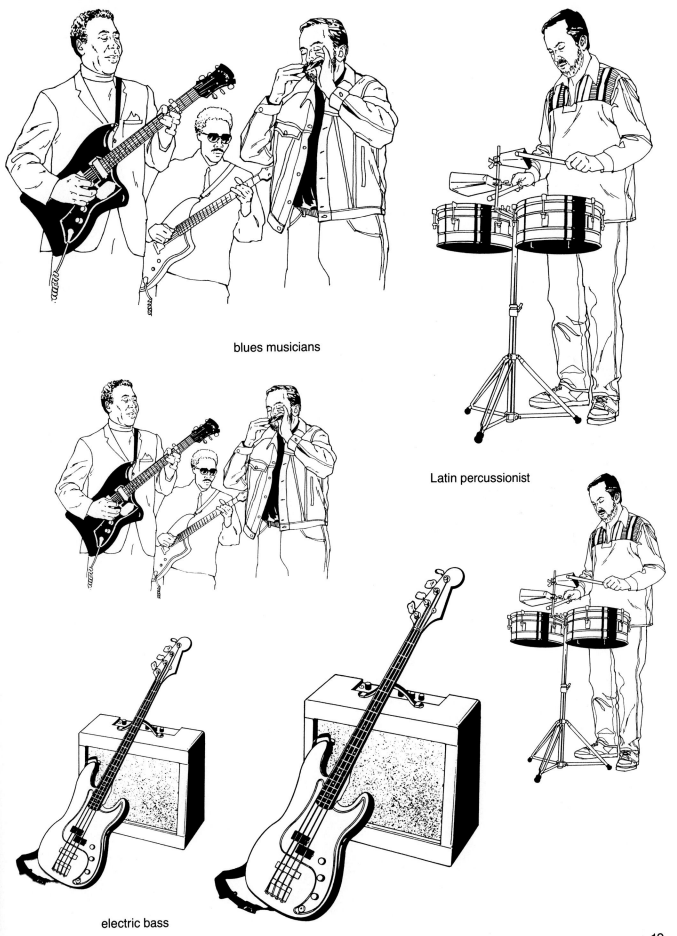

blues musicians

Latin percussionist

electric bass

double-bass player

rhythm-and-blues vocalists

electronic keyboardist

country musicians

klezmer clarinetist

trumpet

bagpiper

bass drummer (marching band)

alto saxophone

female vocalists

soprano saxophone

pianist

double bass

male vocalist

acoustic guitarist

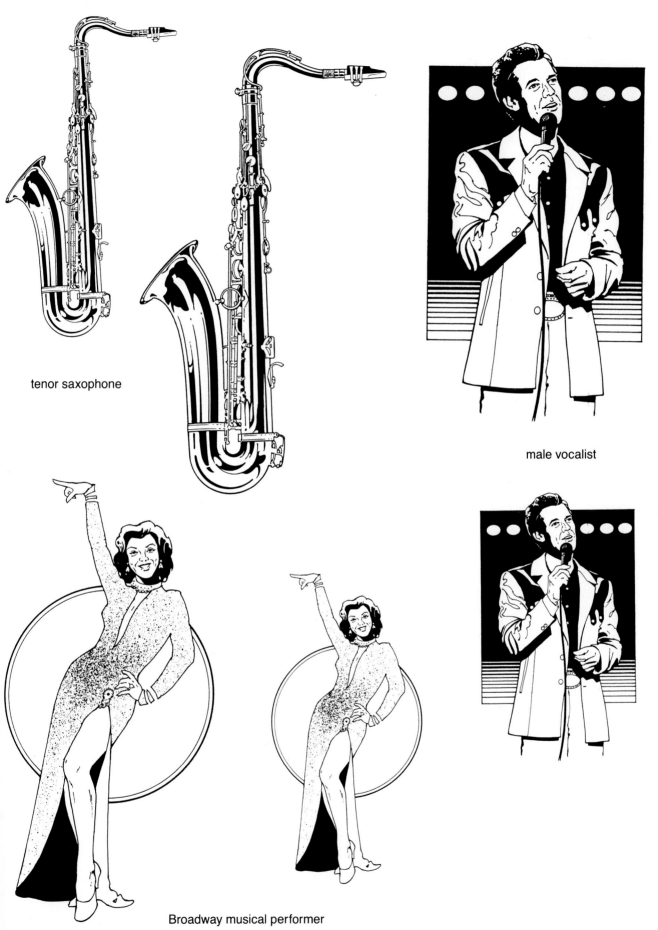

tenor saxophone

male vocalist

Broadway musical performer

trombonist

flutist

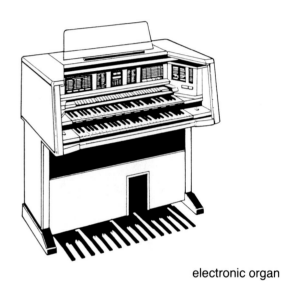

electronic organ

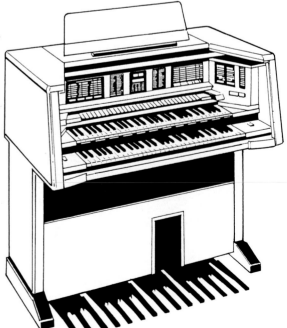

soul musicians

country fiddler

baby grand piano

female vocalist

glockenspiel

bugle players (marching band)

trombonist

clarinetist

drum set

Tex Mex accordionist

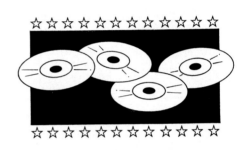

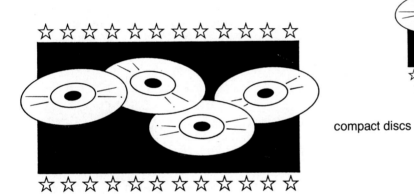

compact discs

conga drummer

male vocalist/guitarist

tuba player (marching band)

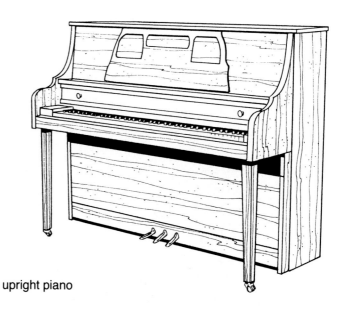

upright piano

electric bassist

baritone saxophonist

rock guitarist

32